Butterfly Prose

Crystal Anderson

BookLeaf
Publishing

Presentation by *BookLeaf Publishing*

Web: www.bookleafpub.com

E-mail: info@bookleafpub.com

ISBN: 9789363302884

First edition 2024

Dedication

I dedicate this book to God the Father, Son and
Holy Spirit

I also dedicate this book to my late Parents,
Gladwyn and Marilyn Richardson

My Aunties, Nell, Marlene, Lofay and Ilys
Richardson

My Parents showed me unconditional love in a
loving family structure

My Aunties were very instrumental in my life
with their hospitality strong ethic and love

Acknowledgement

I would like to express my sincere gratitude to all these individuals for mentoring and supporting me in this project.

Larrita Adderely (for the push), Apostle London, Pastor Burchall, Dr. Althea Winifred, Dr. Eugenia Robinson Loban, Rev. Emily Gail Dill, Apostle Kelly (for the prophecy) Neletha Butterfield, Sandra Spanswick, Sarah Fellows, Nieces Taylor & Candice and late cousin Gwen Smith

To every woman on this earth, you are a beautiful flower...

that has been created by God
You are here to beautify the earth
To bring love, joy, wisdom and balance
You are not here to be degraded in treatment
of character of any type of abuse
Verbal, Physical and Mental
You are a beautiful flower!

Are you in a trap?
Breathe!!
"Inhale and Exhale"
Get out!!
Don't hesitate, it's your life at stake!

Feeling Free

Barriers are removed
I'm lifted from low valleys, loosed,
delivered and not bound

The Bell Has Rung!

You Have Made the Change!

You are the protagonist
(major leaders) Footman
that has rung the bell to open doors
for Reform

I am proud of you
Proud of picking up the Baton from
Martin Luther King Jr.

You have awaken the Nation and the World

Cry out Loud!
Spare Not!

Black Lives Matter!
All Lives Matter!

This is our space in Time
You can't stop until new amendments are
done in the Law books

The Bell has rung....

Global Leaders

Leaders of the Nation

Black Men & Women of Power

You are the movers and shakers!

Push through the glass ceilings of Injustice!

Until Justice is rewritten in the United States Law books!

Equal Justice is for All!

Black Lives Matter
All Lives Matter

United We Stand
Divided We Fall

Calm the chaos of injustice!

Make our Families Whole again with God!

The Little Fish Said,

to the Big Fish
"How do I tread through these waters?
The Big Fish said, **"Carefully!"**

The little fish said…

CHURCH BABIES

God's glory is on them
Some are seasoned before their time for
wisdom
For God's purpose and glory on this earth
Receive them with joy
For they are God's blessings
God's Heartbeat!

Church Babies

Now Is The Time Body

Time? Now? Body?

Talking to the Body of Christ……yes you!
Daughters, Sons, Queens and Kings
To take your rightful place!
To stand….stand up, walk, bend, touch, see,
embrace and resist
Time…Queen to stand up to righteousness
Now….King walk your family to wholeness
Body….To bend, be flexible when things
don't go your way
"For My thoughts are not your thoughts, Nor
are your ways My ways," says
the LORD Isaiah 55: 8-9
Touch God's bountiful blessings, live in
abundance
See his provisions and needs of the people
Embrace the love I have for you
Embrace the unbraceable that have not seen
My love John 3:16
Resist sin in all its attributes; don't second
guess or compromise
Detox! Move out!
Talking to the Body of Christ
You…are…Me!

Written by the pen of
Be Encouraged Today

Crystal
June 3rd, 2018

Look into the Window, the Window of your Mind

Baby Boy, look into the Window of your Mind
Baby Boy remember your Mother's Morals, Teaching and Love
Baby Boy remember your Grandmother's hand how she guided you young with instruction
Baby Boy you are a Man Now
Walk as a Man of Integrity
STOP THE VIOLENCE!!
EVOLVE!!

Laughter is medicine for the Soul

To my friend who always made me laugh

Seeing your smile that was so full of joy
We laughed

Meetup after work to have a bite to eat
somewhere
We laughed and giggled

Seeing how proper you ride your bike
I laughed

Sharing our life's challenges of mistakes and
triumphs of how
God brought us through
We praised God!
We laughed

Sitting on my plastic couch which was about
to give way and collapse
while sending videos to loved ones and
friends
We laughed out loud

"Just before I left the island for vacation,"
He said, "he felt a little stressed."
I said, "Don't go there!" **We hugged and**
We laughed

This Tribute is to one of my best friends
The late Marvin Washington

My late best friend Marvin

Post Cup Match Summary

The little red mouse said to the big blue church mouse
"Do you think Somerset won because of all those silly jokes and
bragging that St. George's fans did over the years?
The big blue church mouse said well…yes, certainly yes, they were full
of it! They kept saying their silly jokes and bragging.
This time their bragging did not help!!
Who has the last laugh now!!!???

The Willow Egg

the willow egg is blue with gold dust
sprinkled around it
the willow egg looks pretty on the outside
but
when cracked, it's rotten to the cure
All that glitters is not gold
Use wisdom!!

Ertugrul

My beautiful handsome cat
His name stands for Justice and Peace
His Coat is a mirror of Love

Ertugrul lives in a Sandys neighborhood
along with cats Blaze, Ginger, Marley and
Oreo
RIP Tonto.
They all get along and sometimes they fight
Just as us humans, sometimes we quarrel
Their coat colors mirror their personalities
Blaze is all gray, the friendliest cat I have
ever met
Ginger is all ginger, he likes to start fights
sometimes
Marley is all black with a small touch of
white
Oreo looks like an oreo cookie, sometimes
he gets moody
Tonto was a stunning snow-white cat with a
touch of gray on his tail.

My Cat…

Spiritual Work out Boot Camp

Prayer-
IT IS YOU THAT HAS BLESSED US, WE
THANK YOU
You are our rock, sword, shield and strong
tower
Your right hand establishes us
We clothe ourselves in victorious garments
We cast down depression and oppression
and lay it at your feet
We bind satanic oppression, depression
Loose us
BY YOU WE RUN THROUGH TROOPS
BY YOU WE LEAP OVER WALLS
You are the God that guards us with strength

Motivation Speak
Eric Thomas- ET
How bad do you want it?
What do you want?
No excuse, living up to your fullest potential
Victor, not a Victim
Winners spread
Winners win!
Stop finding excuses

Scriptures
Psalms 46:1 -3 refuge & strength
Proverbs 18:10 name of the Lord
Nehemiah 8:10 joy of the Lord

Crown

"Nadia!"
"Yes Father?"
She turned around suddenly with her black
shiny locks that swished in the air
You are forgetting your CROWN!....here!!
Nadia leaped.....into the air and **grabbed
her CROWN......AND PLACED IT ON
HER HEAD**

Don't forget you are representing this Tribe
of this Nation!
Yes, Father, it's my honor!

Spiritual Fiction Story
from the Sermonette of "Girl Fix Your
Crown"
Written by the pen
of Sandysgirl

When we put on the helmet of salvation, we
can avoid sinful thoughts and understand
what is good and true.
Romans 12: "Do not conform to the pattern
of this world, but be transformed by the
renewing of your mind.

Then you will be able to test and approve what God's will is—his good, pleasing and perfect will.
Wear your Crown with Honor!!
Girl, fix your Crown!

CROWN

The book of John 19:2
So Pilate took Jesus and had him whipped. The soldiers, **having braided a crown from thorns, set it on his head**
Key Word- Punishment
Key Word- Braided

Braided: Intertwining punishment & falsely accused
It may come in different facets
Facets: One side of something many-sided

Mathew 27:29
The soldiers assigned to the governor took Jesus into the governor's palace and got the entire brigade together for some fun
Key Word- Mocked

John 19:5
Pilate went back out again and said to them, "I present him to you, but I want you to know that I do not find him guilty

of any crime." Just then Jesus came out wearing the thorn crown and purple robe. Key word- Displayed

Punishment, Braided, Mocked and Displayed

When you go through your storms, tests, trials, unforeseen circumstances, uncharted territory and extreme conditions
Hold on to God's unchaining hand
Your tests, challenges, and struggles are your training grounds
He will give you counsel in the midst of your storms, tests etc...

God's will never changes. Psalm 33:11 **says**, "The counsel of the **Lord** stands forever, the plans of His heart to all generations." His Word **is** Timeless and His Promises are Everlasting!

Use your authority to break through the storms: Bible, Prayer, Praise, Worship, Decree & Declare, Power of Agreement and Standing Still in Silence.

Confession: I excel in productivity and the love of God!

Prayer: As Citizens of the Kingdom of GOD your thoughts will not be hijacked for you have the mind of Christ
which is his thoughts, his feelings and his purpose, this word will stick to your Spirit and produce divine fruit for God's honor and Glory! Amen!!

Ms. LadyBug

Your Red & Black is worn
with dignity and humility
Jacqueline

Pretty Little Feet

Isaiah 52:7
How beautiful on the mountains are the feet
of him
who brings good news, who announces
peace and brings good news of happiness,
who announces salvation and says to Zion
your God reigns.
Pretty Little Feet
Pretty Little Feet
Who would have thought this little Girl
named Blanche
with Pretty Little Feet would one day preach
God's word with
power and love.
God knew and saw your Pretty Little Feet.

Float like a Butterfly

Sting like a Bee

These were the famous words of the great Muhammad Ali.
The Butterfly is a creature that was created by God I believe to beautify the earth.
They help to pollinate flowers and are good environmental indicators.
One of the resident Butterflies in Bermuda is the Monarch Butterfly.

Taylor Crystal Ralph, you are that Monarch Butterfly!
Monarch is a sovereign head of state. A king or queen that governs in wisdom.
I say these words to you Queen Taylor, today: don't float but soar! Soar! Like an eagle with your
Monarch Butterfly wings. Go up higher above the turbulence of life's tests, circumstances, and trials.

When you have reached the level plane in the clouds float, rest, rest, reflect, and learn from the tests,
circumstances, and trials. Take in wisdom, it is always there waiting for you to go to a resilient level in

life's journey.

God has designed you uniquely to beautify the earth with your presidential gifts and voice.
Last of all, be your own indicator to detox from toxic environments that will try to cripple you,
stop you from soaring, floating, resting and taking in wisdom.
Sting like the Bee!
Arise Monarch Queen Butterfly, Teach Us!

This Prose Poem is dedicated to my niece Taylor Crystal Ralph that graduated from New York
University, New York, USA, 2018

STARDUST

Stardust is a magical or charismatic quality
or feeling
You are an awesome brother!
You bring a magical feeling of brotherly
love everyday
On your Earth Day today, may you embrace
God's beautiful sea of aquamarine
The sea where you train, teach and get your
victories as a professional world-class
athlete
May you continue to be that Stardust that
shines bright of love and inspiration to us all
Inspiration that we can achieve our goals of
living a healthy life while having fun

Spiritual Insight from Royal Gazette Newspaper

March 20th, 2019

God gave me Spiritual insight regarding the Grey Seal, Bat, Cargo ships The Oleander, Oleander 111 & Blue Birds.

The Grey Seal was believed to be swept off course from the changes of the Gulf Stream; it was found in Bermuda.
It was out of his environment
The Grey Seal is a familiar sight around all the British Isles.
Spiritually sometimes in life you become swept off course/out of your environment, out of whack and your frequency connection with God is a little fuzzy
However, the Bible says he will never leave you or forsake you, Hebrews 13:5
God will not allow your foot to slip
He will not suffer thy foot to be moved: he that keepeth thee will not slumber
The Lord is your protector, and he won't go to sleep or let you stumble
He will take you to a safe place
Psalms 46
God is our refuge and strength
Therefore we will not fear!

The Grey Seal was injured and came to safety
God will heal our wounds….
I am the Lord that healeth thee
Exodus 15:26

The Bat

A Bat is always in a dark place
The Bat was found in Daylight; it came out from its natural environment, which is a cave.
I believe it was injured as well
Spiritually, we need to walk in the Light!
Matthew 4:16
"The People who were sitting in darkness saw a great light and those who were sitting in the land and shadow of death, upon
them a light dawned."
In the land of Zebulun and of Naphtali, beside the sea, beyond the Jordan River in Galilee where so many Gentiles live.
The people who sat in darkness have seen a great light and those who lived in the land where death casts its shadow, a light has shined
The Message Bible says they watched the sun come up
I John 1 : 6-8
If we say that we have fellowship with him, and walk in darkness, we lie, and do not tell

the truth but if we walk in the light, as he is in the light.
We have fellowship with God.

Cargo Ships

Oleander 111 and The Oleander at Hamilton Harbour
You have heard of the expressions out with the Old and In with the New
Spiritually and Prophetically God wants to do a new thing in your life but you have to let him do it
Let him take full charge of your life
Get out of the way!

Blue Birds

On East Shore Lane, Sandys I had seen three Blue birds
They say when you see them it's the beginning of Spring
Spiritually, God wants to do a new thing in your life
Isaia 43:19
I will do a new thing, now it shall spring forth; shall you not know it?
I will even make a road in the wilderness and rivers in the desert.

My Sheep hear my voice, and I know them, and they follow me:

John 10:27

The sheep recognizes the voice of the shepherd, the voice of the shepherd, the one who feeds them, guides them, and protects them.
The sheep have learned to trust the Shepard.
As a shepherd ensures the safety of his sheep, Jesus shields his people from everlasting damage.
Sheep in Greek is provato.

Hospitality

You are Ambassadors
Being a Team Player is vital!
When you say not in my job description,
you don't win
Bad attitudes, you don't win: attitudes are
contagious, is yours worth catching?
Seeing the vision with cooperation is the key
for success!

DESTINY + FAITH

Jasmine and I met waitress Destiny at Olive Garden
@ Trimm Gym wet met Faith in the Sauna (
Steam room)
Faith: causes you to operate in the next level of thinking
and you can reach your Destiny on your Spiritual journey

Jasmine and I took care of our bodies by relaxing in the
massage chairs, sauna and jacuzzi after ministering in the
dance on Sunday at Kingdom Seekers Church in Memphis

March 27th, 2022

www.ingramcontent.com/pod-product-compliance
Lightning Source LLC
LaVergne TN
LVHW010933200726
843509LV00013B/2204